GENUINE

BECOMING A
REAL TEENAGER

C.B. MARTIN

WITH
WARREN W. WIERSBE

D0897179

Genuine: Becoming a real teenager

© CB Martin, 2012

All rights reserved. Except as may be permitted by the Copyright Act, no part of this publication may be reproduced in any form or by any means without prior permission from the publisher.

Published by 10Publishing, a division of 10ofThose Limited.

ISBN: 9781906173708

This books is based largely on Warren W. Wiersbe's book *Be a Real Teenager*, which was published some years ago. With his written permission we have extended, modernised and developed the text to bring it to a new generation. We are deeply grateful for his kind support.

Scripture taken from the HOLY BIBLE, NEW INTERNATIONAL VERSION®. Copyright © 1973, 1978, 1984 Biblica. Used by permission of Zondervan. All rights reserved.

The "NIV" and "New International Version" trademarks are registered in the United States Patent and Trademark Office by Biblica. Use of either trademark requires the permission of Biblica.

Design and Typeset by: Design Chapel / www.design-chapel.com

Printed by: CPI Group, (UK) Ltd, Croydon, CR0 4YY

10Publishing, a division of 10ofthose.com

9D Centurion Court, Leyland, PR25 3UQ, England

Email: info@10ofthose.com

Website: www.10ofthose.com

Reprinted 2015.

CONTENTS

ACKNOWLEDGEMENTS

For John.

With huge thanks for introducing me
to Jesus when I was 18,
and everything since.

And for Toby, Dexter and Harry
(1 Cor. 16:13,14)

INTRODUCTION

In the opening programme of the UK TV series *Young Apprentice*, Lord Alan Sugar says to the 16 and 17 years olds gathered in his boardroom:

You are young. Don't try and pretend that you know it all, because, believe me, it will be embarrassing.

These people are smart, ambitious, and some have already successfully started their own businesses. But they are still teenagers. They are not kids, but they are not yet adults. The most successful (and likeable) contestants are the ones who don't pretend to be something they are not. They have huge potential, but at the same time are willing to learn.

Of course, others are arrogant, paying no attention to their teammates and failing to listen to Lord Sugar's advice. They confuse pig-headedness with leadership and think they know it all already.

Which is the genuine teenager? A genuine teenager today will be a genuine adult tomorrow. The teenage years are a wonderful opportunity, a bridge between childhood and the responsibilities of adult life; a time of transition, to prepare and invest for tomorrow. But it's also a time to enjoy; without rushing ahead to the next thing and failing to make the most of today. But that is not the image sold by the media. A young person is worth millions just as long as they live up to the fake image of a teenager created by the advertisers; they were being prepared for it even as a pre-teen when they were marketed Bratz Dolls and 'No Parents Allowed' signs for their bedroom door.

The teen market for mobile phones, music, fashion and entertainment is massive. Being a teenager is no longer about preparing for adulthood but playing at being an adult; being part of a culture isolated from the real world. The message is all fun with no responsibility, and spending plenty of money along the way.

In *The Last Battle*, the final book in the Narnia series, we find that one of the characters, Susan, has lost all interest in the world of Narnia in her eagerness to grow up. Her life is all about parties, new clothes and lipstick. If the Narnia books were written today, perhaps Susan would have been too preoccupied with fake tanning, Botox and the latest reality TV show to have any time for Narnia!

Today's teenager wants all the trappings of adulthood but isn't ready for the consequences. Playing at being an adult means fake ID for underage drinking and clubbing, buying more and more clothes and gadgets they don't need, sex when they want with who they want. But when this sort of teenager comes face to face with debt, unplanned pregnancy, heartbreak, alcohol addiction or yet another trip to A&E, they are ill-equipped to deal with the fall-out.

The genuine teenager values their teen years, making the most of them, investing in them as they prepare to become an adult. Used wisely, they will be fruitful and fun. Used poorly, they can make a mess of their adult lives before they have even started.

This book aims to share some basic Bible principles which can make your teenage years a success not a failure. We will see genuine teenagers from the Bible in action, and learn from their successes and failures how to be a genuine teenager. We'll see how God turns Joseph's dreams into reality, and how David's teenage years prepare him for a royal future. A look at Daniel will show what it means to be a transformer, not a conformer. Mary demonstrates life-changing faith. Timothy helps us to see what it means to be a young and faithful leader. Not forgetting, of course, the most genuine, perfect teenager of all, Jesus Christ, and we'll start to see how all the others point to Him. We will see from these case studies that the genuine teenager accepts who they are, understands themself,lives with purpose and knows they can't make it on their own.

THIS BOOK AIMS TO SHARE SOME BASIC BIBLE PRINCIPLES WHICH CAN MAKE YOUR TEENAGE YEARS A SUCCESS NOT A FAILURE.

If you're a teen, have you recognized that these are transition years? Like learning to ride a bike with stabilizers or drive a car with your instructor on the dual controls, you can learn to be an adult in a safe environment. If you invest in your teenage years, you will reap the rewards as you enter into adulthood. Do you understand yourself? Everything is changing in your world, physically and emotionally, relationally and even spatially as you prepare to leave home and start to relate to your parents as an adult. The genuine teenager might be knocked sideways but not off balance by these changes, because they understand why they are happening and where they are headed.

Do you live with purpose? Are you *using* your teen years, not just *enjoying* them? It has often been said that what you are going to be, you are becoming right now.

Perhaps most counter-culturally of all, the genuine teenager knows that they can't go it alone. You won't hear them shouting, 'Leave me alone, and let me run my own life!' They know that they need their family, friends and God to make a success of their teen years as they seek the best examples to follow, the best advice to listen to, and the best possible goals to aim for.

DO YOU LIVE WITH PURPOSE? ARE YOU USING YOUR TEEN YEARS, NOT JUST ENJOYING THEM?

Don't waste your teenage years – they are valuable and special. Be what you are. A genuine teenager, like the ones we'll find in the Bible and in the pages of this book, is something special. Someone God is shaping and using for His glory.

CB Martin

THE DREAMER: JOSEPH

You turn on the TV, and hear Voiceover Man's deep, mystic tones over some vaguely apocalyptic music: 'They came in their thousands . . . all with one dream . . .'

Whether that dream involved singing bad cover versions with a troupe of bizarrely dressed backing dancers is another matter entirely!

What's your dream? Whether it revolves around winning the FA Cup, or topping the charts, chances are it's based on one thing – success. There's nothing wrong with having dreams. If we didn't dare to dream, then many great things would never have happened. But dreams without discipline and hard work can turn into nightmares if they come true at all.

Every serious sportsperson, athlete, singer and dancer knows the value of discipline. Without it you don't stand a chance of succeeding in your chosen field. On the other hand, pretty much every reality TV show is selling us the lie that you can be a success without the hard work. Instant fame and fortune. Being plucked out of nowhere to become the next star. But how do people cope with the success they haven't worked for? On the whole, badly.

One look at the celeb magazines will show you the train wrecks that follow.

Dreams alone never lead to success. And this principle has no better example than Joseph, the teenage dreamer. You know the guy – Technicolor Dreamcoat and all that. The Bible gives us a very detailed portrait of Joseph, beginning when he is only 17. You can split his exciting life into four stages: the Dreamer, the Worker, the Prisoner, and the Ruler. As you read his story, you will see God making a young man's dreams into reality – but only when he submits himself to the disciplines God sends his way.

DREAMS ALONE NEVER LEAD TO SUCCESS.

Check out Genesis 37:1–36 and chapter 39. It's a gripping tale of sibling rivalry, attempted murder, slavery, sexual temptation, and prison. Read on to the end of chapter 41 to get the whole story.

At the end of chapter 37, Joseph the Dreamer is in a pretty bad way. His death has been faked by his brothers, his dad is distraught, and he's been sold into slavery. But it's certainly not the end of the story. God eventually turned those early dreams of Joseph's into reality, but perhaps not in the way the teenage Joseph was expecting. Let's not forget that it took God thirteen years to make something out of Joseph.

Imagine for a moment that God did that for you. What is your greatest dream? What do you think God's plan is for you? Psalm 37:4 tells us: 'Delight yourself in the LORD and he will give you the desires of your heart.' If you let God discipline you as He did Joseph, then He will use you for His glory.

Joseph's early years don't exactly make you warm to the guy. He's a spoilt brat, and up until the point where they actually try to murder him (and maybe even then), I'm guessing your sympathies are largely with his brothers. Younger brothers are annoying at the best of times, and when this one is so obviously favoured over everyone else by his father, it makes for a pretty dysfunctional family. Joseph doesn't have to work like his brothers do, and just to make that point absolutely crystal clear, his father gives him a fancy coat with long sleeves showing he is a ruler not a worker. To add to his general annoyingness, Joseph seems to spend most of his time spying on his brothers. The dreams he shares about his father, mother and brothers bowing down to him don't exactly go down well, to put it mildly.

If God had left Joseph to his father's pampering, he would never have amounted to anything. But God had some amazing plans for Joseph. He would help rescue God's people, which in turn would eventually lead to the safe arrival of Jesus Christ into our world. Joseph really would become a true success and a great ruler, but that would never happen whilst he was being spoilt by his father. God was going to have to make some drastic changes to Joseph's life.

Now, I guess it's easy for us to agree in our heads that God uses tough circumstances to shape us and make us more like Jesus. We can all sign up to those great promises in Romans 8:28,29:

And we know that in all things God works for

the good of those who love him, who have been called according to his purpose. For those God foreknew he also predestined to be conformed to the likeness of his Son, that he might be the firstborn among many brothers.

But when you're in the middle of those difficult times, do you really trust that God is using them for your good? God used three disciplines to make a man out of Joseph, and He wants to use these same disciplines in your life today.

Discipline number one was the . . .

DISCIPLINE OF SERVICE

Joseph went from riches to rags as God arranged for him to be sold as a slave. Gone was the beautiful ruler's coat; instead, he had to wear a slave's tunic. His lazy, manicured hands were suddenly given the hardest possible work. Talk about going from one extreme to the other. Picture the scene:

A strong Egyptian soldier, obviously an officer, steps up to the slave trader. 'I need a boy to work in my house.'

'Fine, fine!' replies the dealer. 'I have a Hebrew lad here – not very strong, but he has potential.'

They bargain over the price while Joseph stands by helplessly, just beginning to realize that he is no longer a human being; he is now a piece of property.

The captain approaches Joseph. 'I am your new master. I am Potiphar, captain of Pharaoh's guard. What is your name?"

Sullenly, the boy answers, 'Joseph.'

Slap! The soldier's rough hand tears across Joseph's tender cheek. 'Joseph what?'

The lad feels his burning cheek and replies, 'Joseph, *sir.*'

'That's better. I can see that you don't know what it is to have respect for your elders; and chances are you don't want to work. Well, we can change that!' And, giving Joseph a rough shove, he starts back home.

You can see why God had to use the discipline of service in Joseph's life, because that was the way He would teach Joseph the important lessons he needed to learn before his dreams became reality. For one thing, Joseph had to learn humility, and there is no better way to learn that vital lesson than through service. A teenager who has no respect for his elders will never be used by God. Peter puts it this way:

Young men, in the same way be submissive to those who are older. All of you, clothe yourselves with humility towards one another, because, 'God opposes the proud but gives grace to the humble.' Humble yourselves, therefore, under God's mighty hand, that he may lift you up in due time. (1 Pet. 5:5,6)

God had to literally strip Joseph of his flashy coat and

clothe him with a slave's tunic so that Joseph might learn to be 'clothed with humility'. A teenager who is not willing to work, to take orders, to lower themselves to do humble jobs, will never experience a promotion from God in the future.

While weekend jobs have downsides, especially if they mean missing church or youth group, they can teach you a lot about service. You're usually the bottom of the heap and have to do decidedly unglamorous jobs such as washing up, shelf stacking, or dealing with grumpy customers. Even if the only jobs you do are washing the family car, taking out the rubbish, or washing up at home, you can use those circumstances to learn humility, respect for others and willing service. Those things are way more valuable that the minimum wage or your weekly allowance. You are getting ready for adulthood. So allow God to discipline you.

As part of learning the discipline of service, Joseph had to learn the lesson of diligence.

Proverbs 12:24 puts it this way: 'Diligent hands will rule, but laziness ends in slave labour.' Proverbs 22:29 says: 'Do you see a man skilled in his work? He will serve before kings'.

Diligence simply means faithfulness to do the job properly. You don't find many conscientious people around. Most people's attitude to work is, 'What can I get away with?' or 'What is the bare minimum?' Do you think that explains why many teens never see their dreams become reality? Living in an age of instant gratification means very few of us know what it means to really work – to start the job and do it properly until it's finished.

Dreams without discipline become nightmares; and the first discipline Joseph experienced was service. He had to learn how to work.

The second discipline was . . .

DISCIPLINE OF SELF-CONTROL

Check out the details in Genesis 39:6–18.

Like Joseph, most of us are no strangers to sexual temptation. Physically speaking, as you hit adolescence your body is a cocktail of hormones waiting to explode. It's incredibly easy to fall into sexual sin – in your mind and behaviour. Whilst some things become easier to deal with as you get older and more mature in your thinking, the temptation never goes away.

Today's teenagers, whilst no worse than any previous generation, are bombarded by sexual temptation in a way that no other group of teenagers throughout history has been. Pornography is only a click away on the Internet. Sexual images are there on your mobile phone. Even TV, advertising billboards and magazines are blatant about things which only a generation ago would have been top shelf, 'over-18s only' material.

Why did God allow Joseph to be tempted? So that he might develop the discipline of self-control, because the man who cannot control himself will never be able to control others. God had Joseph marked out to be a great ruler; but he had to prove first of all that he could rule his own body. The reason great rulers such as Samson lost their positions was because they could not control themselves. See what advice Paul gives in 1 Corinthians 9:25–27:

Everyone who competes in the games goes into strict training. They do it to get a crown that will not last; but we do it to get a crown that will last for ever. Therefore I do not run like a man running aimlessly; I do not fight like a man beating the air. No, I beat my body and make it my slave so that after I have preached to others, I myself will not be disqualified for the prize.

Like any sportsperson, Paul knew the value of self-control and discipline. The celebrity who enters a marathon on a whim with no prior training will find their body gives up on them, no matter how much they want to keep going.

How did Joseph gain victory over the temptations of the flesh? The same way you can:

. . . clothe yourselves with the Lord Jesus Christ, and do not think about how to gratify the desires of the sinful nature. (Rom. 13:14)

Flee the evil desires of youth . . . (2 Tim. 2:22)

Joseph deliberately stayed away from Potiphar's wife; and when she did tempt him, he ran the other way.

Picture a man walking down a street. He falls into a large hole. It takes him most of the day to get out of it. The next day he walks down the street again, and falls into the hole once more. It takes him most of the morning to escape. The third day he walks down the street and falls into the hole yet again. This time, it only takes him a few hours to get out. The next day he walks down a different street.

Take whatever steps you need to, to avoid temptation. Joseph was not ashamed to run away from it. If you know you are weak in a particular area, then avoid it. Walk a different route to school that doesn't take you past that shop window. Put accountability software on your computer to stop you visiting certain sites. Buy a mobile package without (shock horror!) Internet capabilities, if that's a stumbling point for you. Get a friend to ask you whether you've been reading those books or watching that TV programme.

The discipline of self-control is important to your future. If you fail to learn control today, you will never know real success tomorrow. Remember, you are not alone in this. Talk to a Christian friend, youth leader or pastor if you're really struggling in this area. [1]

REMEMBER, YOU ARE NOT ALONE IN THIS.

Despite all this, the two disciplines of service and self-control were not enough; God had to use a third discipline to make a man out of this boy.

DISCIPLINE OF SUFFERING

Nobody enjoys suffering, and young people especially dislike being restricted and confined. Yet God permitted Joseph to remain a prisoner for over two years. Why? Because He had a wonderful purpose in mind, as Psalm 105:17–19 explains:

[God] sent a man before them – Joseph, sold as a slave. They bruised his feet with shackles, his neck was put in irons, till what he foretold came to pass, till the Word of the Lord proved him true.

One thing Joseph learned while he waited in prison, all the time knowing he was not guilty, was patience. He also learned to trust God's Word. Satan must have said to Joseph 'Whatever happened to those dreams? What happened to God's promises to you?' On the surface of things, Joseph had every reason to doubt. But in prison Joseph received two blessings, faith and patience, and those are things every teenager needs to learn if they want to see their God-given dreams become reality.

Hebrews 6:12 urges us to 'imitate those who through faith and patience inherit what has been promised'. James also reminds us to 'Consider it pure joy, my brothers, whenever you face trials of many kinds, because you know that the testing of your faith develops perseverance. Perseverance must finish its work so that you may be mature and complete, not lacking anything' (Jas. 1:2–4).

Unfortunately, impatience is almost seen as a virtue in our society; our TV packages and gadgets enable us to fast forward the adverts; we can stream films straight to our phone or computer without needing to queue at the cinema or hire a DVD or Blu-ray. Credit cards promise that you can have it all now without having to wait and save. And this impatience is particularly endemic among teenagers – what are you impatient for? To have more freedom? Stay out later? Find a girl/boyfriend? Have sex? Learn to drive? Leave school? Leave home?

There is all the difference in the world between growing older and growing up. The Christian teenager who has experienced the discipline of suffering knows how to trust God's promises and wait. They know that faith and patience will make their dreams come true.

Christian patience means the difference between a delicious home-cooked full-on Sunday roast and a soggy motorway services sandwich. One satisfies – the other is quickly over and invariably disappointing.

CHRISTIAN PATIENCE MEANS THE DIFFERENCE BETWEEN A DELICIOUS HOME-COOKED FULL-ON SUNDAY ROAST AND A SOGGY MOTORWAY SERVICES SANDWICH. ONE SATISFIES – THE OTHER IS QUICKLY OVER AND INVARIABLY DISAPPOINTING.

Joseph started off life like most of us with three big 'I' problems. His worst 'I' problem was *importance*; Joseph was proud and God had to make him a servant to teach him humility. His second problem was *impurity*; he needed to learn the discipline of self-control. His third problem was *impatience*; the discipline of suffering took care of that.

God took thirteen years to train Joseph and make his dreams into reality. And if this all seems a long time ago, remember how crucial Joseph was – it was Joseph who saved the Jewish nation in a time of famine, and it was through that nation that God gave us His Saviour, Jesus. Psalm 37:4 says: 'Delight yourself in the Lord and he will give you the desires of your heart.'

God has a perfect plan for your life; but before He can use you, He must discipline you, and this discipline starts in your teenage years. You'll never regret learning this key truth early on in your life. Remember God's plan from Romans 8:28,29? He is going to make you like Jesus! So take heart when he disciplines you:

My son, do not make light of the Lord's discipline,

and do not lose heart when he rebukes you,

because the Lord disciplines those he loves,

and he punishes everyone he accepts as a son.
(Heb. 1:5,6)

Let God put His dreams into your heart. Then let Him turn those dreams into reality as you learn the meaning of service, self-control and suffering.

MAKE IT REAL

What's your greatest dream?

What would be the best thing about being more like Jesus?

What's your attitude towards suffering, service and self-control? Has Joseph's story changed that? Which one do you need to pray about?

NOTE

1. For more help in this area, try reading Tim Chester's book *Captured by a Better Vision* (Nottingham: IVP, 2010).

THE FUTURE KING: DAVID

When Kate Middleton married Prince William, there were a whole series of articles and online stories about her life. They were mostly focused on her good looks, her sporting abilities and her academic achievements. One article was entitled 'A Princess in Waiting'.

David may not have attended a top public school, been captain of any sports teams or gone to a prestigious university but, unknown to him, his teenage years were also preparing him for life as royalty. You might think you know all about the shepherd boy who became king, but go ahead and read his story now in 1 Samuel 16:1 – 17:54 and then 2 Samuel 5:4,5.

Of course, the most amazing thing about David is that he was Jesus' great-great-great etc. grandfather, and we can see many patterns in his life and kingship that foreshadow and predict that perfect King. That includes the three helpful principles we'll see in David's teenage years. Firstly, we start as servants before God makes us rulers. Secondly, we start with a few things before God gives us many things. Finally, we start with work before we experience joy.

PRINCIPLE 1: WE START AS SERVANTS BEFORE GOD MAKES US RULERS

God's pattern has always been to start at the bottom – think back to Joseph. Moses, through whom God gave His Law to Israel, spent forty years as a shepherd before God made him the great leader of Israel. Joshua was Moses' servant before he because his successor. The great prophet Samuel began life cleaning the furniture in the tabernacle (the place of worship in those days). And God doesn't ask His people to do anything He hasn't done Himself – look at Jesus, as described in Philippians 2:6–11. He was God in the flesh, and He humbled Himself to become a servant, for our sakes.

GOD DOESN'T ASK HIS PEOPLE TO DO ANYTHING HE HASN'T DONE HIMSELF

David wasn't too proud to obey his father and stay at home taking care of the sheep. He didn't throw a strop and insist on being able to do everything his older brothers were doing. He knew how to serve. He would never have been a success in the nation if he'd been a failure at home. Spoilt teenagers make frustrated, unsuccessful adults.

PRINCIPLE 2: WE START WITH A FEW THINGS BEFORE GOD GIVES US MANY THINGS

Not having much isn't particularly attractive to most of us – Ryan and Sharpay sing in *High School Musical 3* about 'wanting it all'. Teenage culture, as created by the advertisers, is all about getting more and more stuff. But God's policy is to see how faithful we are with the small things before He entrusts us with much (see Matt. 25:21 – in fact, read the whole story, vv. 14–30).

David didn't start off with much, but because he was faithful in the small things, God entrusted him with bigger ones.

He started with caring faithfully for a few sheep when a teenager, and as an adult God made him king over the whole nation of Israel. David killed a lion and a bear in private, so God permitted him to kill a giant in public. David sang to himself while tending the sheep, and today the whole world sings his songs as recorded in the book of Psalms. As a young man, he faithfully delivered supplies to his brothers on the front line, and as an old man he delivered billions of pounds worth of materials to his son Solomon to build the Temple.

DAVID DIDN'T START OFF WITH MUCH, BUT BECAUSE HE WAS FAITHFUL IN THE SMALL THINGS, GOD ENTRUSTED HIM WITH BIGGER ONES.

God develops our Christian character in the small things. They way you approach an essay deadline today will shape your university career tomorrow. Keeping your temper with an annoying younger brother today will help you deal with a difficult colleague tomorrow. The apostle Paul is able to rejoice even in suffering because 'we know that suffering produces perseverance; perseverance, character; and character, hope. And hope does not disappoint us, because God has poured out his love into our hearts by the Holy Spirit, whom he has given us' (Rom. 5:3–5).

When you remember that God is at work in your life, there is no such thing as a waste of time or a pointless situation – remember he is at work in all things to make us more like Jesus (Rom. 8:28,29).

This leads us to our final principle . . .

PRINCIPLE 3: WE START WITH WORK BEFORE WE EXPERIENCE JOY

The pattern of the Christian life is often suffering before glory – Jesus being the prime example of that. But a lesser pattern can be seen in David's life, and that is work before joy.

Fun without responsibility is ultimately unsatisfying and can end in regret and unhappiness. But one of the things adult life will teach you is that hard work brings a special sort of satisfaction and enjoyment.

I hated maths at school, but I was prouder of my B grade for GCSE maths than any of my better grades because I had worked harder for it. Revising is not fun; practising musical scales is dull; training hard, watching your diet and exercising would not be how you choose to use your time. But good exam results, getting a recording contract or scoring the winning goal are the results. The hard work was an investment in future joy.

A GENUINE TEENAGER, THEN, HAS A SENSE OF PURPOSE.

David knew how to work, and he knew that being faithful today would result in enjoyment tomorrow. You'll recall that spoilt Joseph was a failure at home, largely because his father wouldn't let him work. Once Joseph learned to work, God gave him a kingdom's worth of enjoyment.

A genuine teenager, then, has a sense of purpose; they are faithful in the small things because they know God has bigger things for them in the future, and ultimately a heavenly future full of pure joy.

Also, sometimes we learn more from failures than successes. Have a look at the story of the prodigal son in Luke 15:11–31. Read it all the way through, even if you think you already know it.

If David illustrates God's principles for success, then the prodigal, or runaway, son pictures the world's criteria for success. David and the runaway son are polar opposites in their approach to life, and it's important to recognize the difference.

THE RUNAWAY SON STARTED WITH MANY THINGS AND ENDED WITH NOTHING

Like many of today's teenagers, the runaway son wanted more and more *stuff*. He wanted to enjoy it all now, rather than waiting for his inheritance when his father was dead. He thought that money could buy him friends and happiness. He thought having the latest gadgets, going to the wildest parties, racking up friends and having as many one-night stands as possible would make his life complete.

All too quickly he discovered that these things are worthless without genuine love and relationship. Remember that the father in this parable stands for God. When we want His good gifts but reject Him, it ends in spiritual poverty and disaster.

THE RUNAWAY SON STARTED AS A RULER BUT ENDED UP AS A SERVANT

Ironic, isn't it? The runaway son had everything going for him in his father's house, but when he set out to rule his own life, he ended up as the lowest kind of slave, looking after the pigs. Pigs weren't just smelly, they were 'unclean' animals to the Jewish people.

Be willing to serve now and God will prepare you for greater opportunities tomorrow. Jesus makes this point:

When he noticed how the guests picked the places of honour at the table, he told them this parable: "When someone invites you to a wedding feast, do not take the place of honour, for a person more distinguished than you may have been invited. If so, the host who invited both of you will come and say to you, 'Give this man your seat.' Then, humiliated, you will have to take the least important place. But when you are invited, take the lowest place, so that when your host comes, he will say to you, 'Friend, move up to a better place.' Then you will be honoured in the presence of all your fellow guests. For everyone who exalts himself will be

humbled, and he who humbles himself will be exalted. (Luke 14:7–11)

THE RUNAWAY SON STARTED WITH JOY AND ENDED WITH SORROW

All the runaway son was after when he left home was fun, and lots of it. He thought that joy came from money, parties, physical pleasure, sin, and so-called liberty. He discovered that sin always promises happiness, but delivers tragedy. When Edmund meets the White Witch in C.S. Lewis's *The Lion, the Witch and the Wardrobe*, he stuffs himself with the Turkish delight she gives him. At the time it's the most delicious thing he's ever tasted, but later he starts to feel sick, betrays his own family and becomes the witch's prisoner.

The son who began by saying 'It's no fun at home – I want to leave and have a good time' soon realizes that home is the only place he wants to be. The problem was in his heart, not his home, all along.

THE PROBLEM WAS IN HIS HEART, NOT HIS HOME, ALL ALONG.

The genuine teenager follows David's example and is willing to let God set the agenda for the future. The teenager playing at being an adult just wants everything right here, right now, just like the runaway son. It's obvious which one is the better way to live. Which have you chosen?

MAKE IT REAL

Which way are you living at the moment?

Does looking at David's life help you see things differently? What about looking at Jesus?

Think about something you have really worked for; why was the reward sweeter?

Ask for God's help to take the long-term view when everyone around you is living for the moment. Think of a specific situation when you find that hard, and pray about it.

THE TRANSFORMER: DANIEL

A young man enlisted, and was sent to his regiment. The first night he was in the barracks with about fifteen other young men, who passed the time playing cards and gambling. Before retiring, he fell on his knees and prayed, and they began to curse him and jeer at him and throw boots at him.

So it went on the next night and the next, and finally the young man went and told the chaplain what had taken place, and asked what he should do.

'Well,' said the chaplain, 'you are not at home now, and the other men have just as much right to the barracks as you have. It makes them mad to hear you pray, and the Lord will hear you just as well if you say your prayers in bed and don't provoke them.'

For weeks after the chaplain did not see the young man again, but one day he met him, and asked –

'By the way, did you take my advice?'

'I did, for two or three nights.'

'How did it work?'

'Well,' said the young man, 'I felt like a whipped hound and the third night I got out of bed, knelt down and prayed.'

'Well,' asked the chaplain, 'How did that work?'

The young soldier answered: 'We have a prayer meeting there now every night, and three have been converted, and we are praying for the rest.'[1]

There is an important distinction between the conformer and transformer. A conformer is a person whose life is controlled by pressures from without; a transformer is a person whose life is controlled by power from within.

DANIEL HAD TO DECIDE WHETHER HE WAS GOING TO LET BABYLON CHANGE HIM, OR WHETHER HE WAS GOING TO CHANGE BABYLON.

Daniel had to decide whether he was going to let Babylon change him, or whether he was going to change Babylon.

Take a look at Daniel 1:1–21 to see Daniel's situation and what he did with it.

From what you've read so far, you may be thinking at this point, 'This sounds good; I think I could handle being another Joseph or David.' That's great, but it takes more than Joseph's three disciplines and David's three directions to be a genuine teenager. Daniel, the Jewish teenage refugee who eventually helped rule an empire, illustrates the *decisions* which are necessary to make if you are to succeed.

CONFORMER/ TRANSFORMER?

The first decision Daniel had to make was whether he was going to be a conformer or a transformer. The leaders in Babylon did their best to make Daniel conform. They took him from Jerusalem to Babylon and gave him a new home, a new name, new ideas, a new diet, a new language and even new gods. They wanted to brainwash him and make him one of their puppets. Had Daniel given in to all of this, he would have had a comfortable life with status and security, but he would have missed out on God's great purpose for his life.

Your situation today isn't much different from Daniel's. As a Christian, your 'citizenship is in heaven' (Phil. 3:20), but you're forced to live in this present world until Jesus comes back or God calls you home. But this world is no friend to Christ or Christians, and would like to brainwash you and force you to conform. Unfortunately, many Christian teenagers do conform and consequently miss the best God has for them.

Daniel could have easily argued his way into being a conformer. Like some teenagers today, he could have given several excuses for going along with the pressures being applied. 'Everybody else is doing it!' would have sounded like a valid reason – it appears that Daniel and his three teenage friends were the only ones willing to stand their ground. Of course, Daniel could have said, 'The king commanded it, so I'd better obey.' But remember what the apostles said centuries later: 'We must obey God rather than men' (Acts 5:29). Or, Daniel might have argued, 'We can obey outwardly, but keep our true faith inwardly' rather like the chaplain's advice to the young soldier. Daniel and his friends could have enlisted in a secret resistance movement and perhaps worked underground, except that God has no secret service, and compromise with the enemy is the first step towards defeat.

In the film *Mean Girls*, the character Cady, played by Lindsay Lohan, goes undercover with 'The Plastics', a clique of girls who rule the school. Her aim, spurred on by her friend Janis, is to sabotage the group. But as time goes on, Cady becomes more and more like the self-absorbed, catty clique she hangs with. Anthropologists call it 'going native' when you take on the characteristics of a group you spend time with.

You've probably heard (and perhaps used) all these and more excuses for conforming to the world around you and avoiding the shame and suffering that often comes to a transformer. From a human point of view, Daniel and his three friends were fools for refusing the king's offers. What a great future he had planned for them – free education (no student loan!), fame, security, status, wealth . . . What more could a teenager want?

'WE MUST OBEY GOD RATHER THAN MEN'
(ACTS 5:29).

Despite all this, Daniel chose to be a transformer, and I hope you'll make the same decision. In order to understand what it means to be a transformer, you need to identify the pressures around you that can make you conform, and then see the power God has for you to use in overcoming these pressures.

THE WORLD

I'm sure that many times you've heard people talk about 'the world' or 'worldly Christians'. Or perhaps you've read verses like these in your Bible:

> **Do not love the world or anything in the world. If anyone loves the world, the love of the Father is not in him. For everything in the world – the cravings of sinful man, the lust of his eyes and the boasting of what he has and does – comes not from the Father but from the world.**
> **The world and its desires pass away, but the man who does the will of God lives forever.**
> **(1 John 2:15–17)**

But what does John mean, or any of the other Bible writers, when they talk about 'the world'? Well, the Bible uses the word 'world' in at least three ways. It speaks of the physical world, e.g. 'God who made the world and everything in it' (Acts 17:24), and also the human world: 'For God so loved the world . . .' (John 3:16). But the Bible also speaks of an invisible system, controlled by Satan, that opposes the work of Christ – 'the world'.

This use of 'the world' is found in 1 John 2:15–17, Romans 12:2, John 17:16, and many other places. When the Bible warns you 'Do not love the world' (1 John 2:15) or 'Do not conform any longer to the pattern of this world' (Rom. 12:2), it has this invisible system in mind.

When you hear someone talk about 'the fashion world' or 'the world of sport' you know they are not literally talking about a planet populated by designers or athletes. It's referring to a sphere of influence – people, places, events, plans, and philosophies. Things visible and invisible but real and powerful nonetheless. All around you every single day is this invisible system that the Bible calls 'the world'. As a Christian, you are in the physical and human world, but not in the world system that is out to oppose Christ.

Perhaps a diagram will make this clearer. When you came into this human world, you brought with you a body, mind, and will. All of your abilities, appetites, and achievements are wrapped up in your body, mind, and will. When you became a Christian, the Holy Spirit of God moved into your life and made your body His temple (1 Cor. 6:19,20); so a Christian looks a bit like this:

Now, all around you is the anti-God world system that the Bible calls 'the world'. Daniel had it around him in Babylon, and you have it in Manchester, London, Belfast, Glasgow, Walton-on-the-Naze or wherever you are. So, let's add the world to our diagram:

You'll remember that 1 John 2:16 identifies three pressures that the world exerts against you all the time, pressures that can make you conform to the world and thereby lose your distinctiveness as a Christian. These pressures work on your body ('the cravings' of your sinful self), your mind ('the lust' of your eyes), and your will ('boasting' of what you have and do). Let's add these pressures to our diagram:

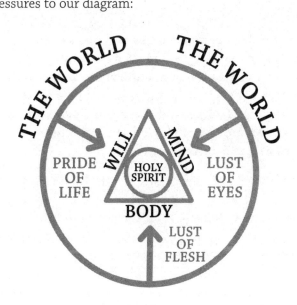

If we turn back to Daniel in Babylon, you'll get some idea of how these pressures work. He faced pressure against his body as the king's servants offered him a new diet, and tempted him with things unlawful for a Jew to eat. The new ideas and 'wisdom' that they taught him exerted pressure against his mind – not unlike modern brainwashing. And the wonderful offers of money and position worked on his will and could have conquered him. Had Daniel given in to these subtle pressures, he would have become a conformer, lost his distinctiveness and power, and never survived the lion's den in his old age (see Dan. 6).

But he didn't give in. Daniel knew the secret of being a transformer, and he knew how to overcome the pressures outside. What is that secret? Have a look at Romans 12:1,2:

> **Therefore, I urge you, brothers, in view of God's mercy, to offer your bodies as living sacrifices, holy and pleasing to God – this is your spiritual act of worship. Do not conform any longer to the pattern of this world, but be transformed by the renewing of your mind. Then you will be able to test and approve what God's will is – his good, pleasing and perfect will.**

Note those two important words, *conform[ed]* and *transformed*. Paul tells us here that any Christian can be a transformer by surrendering themselves to God – body, mind, and will. See how Paul talks of our bodies as 'living sacrifices', our minds being 'renewed', and our wills being brought in line with God's will. That's the meaning of dedication: daily surrendering of body, mind, and will to God for Him to control and use. [2]

So what does that look like? A very wise older lady once said to me that the first thing she did when she woke up was to ask herself, 'Who am I?' No, she hadn't had a particularly heavy night of it, but she needed to remind herself who she was. A child of God, deeply loved, forgiven, and strengthened by Him. Start the day like that and dedicate your body, mind, and will to God. Instead of reaching for your phone or Facebook, why not open your

Bible and allow the Word of God to renew your mind? This means reading it, understanding it, and making it a part of your life. The next step is prayer; try starting all your praises and requests with the same attitude that Jesus had – 'not my will, but yours be done' (Luke 22:42). When you have done this, the indwelling Holy Spirit is in control. (Warning: if this is merely a routine, rather than coming from the heart, there's no point. We need to wholeheartedly ask for God's help every single day).

No sooner do you get out of bed than the world starts putting pressure on you. You might have seen this prayer:

Dear God, so far today, I've done all right. I haven't gossiped. I haven't lost my temper. I haven't been greedy, grumpy, nasty, selfish or overindulgent. I'm very thankful for that. But in a few minutes, God, I'm going to get out of bed; and from then on, I'm probably going to need a lot more help. Amen.

Perhaps the world exerts pressure on your body, trying to get you to live for your physical appetites or encouraging you to use your body as the people of the world do. When you sense that pressure at work, try asking God to take charge of your body: 'Father, it's under Your control.' Then the Spirit on the inside counteracts the pressure on the outside – and you get the victory.

Perhaps the pressure is exerted against your mind, and you're tempted to think the way the world thinks: 'Go ahead and cheat on your coursework – it'll be much quicker and easier! You'll get away with it. Everybody cuts and pastes from Wikipedia.' When you turn your mind over to God by faith, then the power on the inside (the Holy Spirit) counteracts the pressure on the outside, and you overcome that temptation.

Perhaps you're walking down the corridor at school and somebody knocks you into the wall on purpose. That proud will of yours (and we all have one) immediately reacts, and the pressure from the world goes to work, tempting you to lose your temper and shove them back, or tell them what you think of them. Instead, you ask the Spirit to take over, and His power from within counteracts that pressure from without, and you smile and get the victory – and are a better witness to Christ.

This is the simple secret of being a transformer instead of a conformer. It's simple, but it's not easy. Because Daniel surrendered body, mind, and will to God, and spent time daily in the Word of God and prayer (see Dan. 6:1–11; 9:2), he was able to live a godly life in a very ungodly nation. Because he fixed his heart on God and not on the world, God honoured him and made him a genuine success in every way (see Dan. 1:8-20).

WHAT WOULD JESUS DO?

So how does this play out in your world? Right here, right now. What would Jesus do? You've probably seen the 'WWJD' wristbands. But it's not always easy to know the answer. Would Jesus get a tattoo? Have his nose pierced? See an 18 film with his mates, even though he was still underage? Would Jesus go to that party? Would he laugh at that comedian? Download that particular artist onto his MP3 player? Would he wear that?

It's all very well to say don't conform to the world, but

how do we know what is right and wrong, what's OK and what we shouldn't go along with, when it isn't always black and white? How far can a Christian go?

Strange though it may seem, these sorts of questions are not modern ones. The Christians in Corinth had exactly the same sort of worries – check out the book of 1 Corinthians. Of course, the Corinthian Christians weren't facing issues of body piercing or albums with Parental Advisory lyrics, but the Bible deals with principles, not rules and regulations. That's why it's still spot on for us today.

Of course, there are specific rules and warnings in the Bible, but when it comes to the area of questionable things, the Bible lays down principles instead. A specific rule usually applies to a specific situation, while a principle applies and works regardless of the time or circumstance. Some sins, of course, can be named: it's always wrong to cheat, steal, lose your temper, etc. You will find these sins in every culture and civilization. But most of the examples above didn't exist in the same way back then, and so the Bible doesn't mention them. Instead, God gives us basic principles, or tests, that apply just as effectively today as they did in Corinth or Rome twenty centuries ago.

OF COURSE, THERE ARE SPECIFIC RULES AND WARNINGS IN THE BIBLE, BUT WHEN IT COMES TO THE AREA OF QUESTIONABLE THINGS, THE BIBLE LAYS DOWN PRINCIPLES INSTEAD.

If you had been a Christian teenager in Corinth, for example, you would have faced the problem of food being offered to idols (1 Cor. 8). We all know that an idol is not a real god, and that food dedicated to an idol is not contaminated. But there were some Christians at Corinth who were offended when their Christian friends ate meat that had been offered to idols when it was served to them in their friends' houses. (In fact, the cheapest meat in town came from the temple sacrifices).

You might have expected the apostle Paul to have given a heavy 'Thou shalt not!' in this situation, but instead he offers four spiritual principles for them to apply to their own lives. These four principles answer the question, 'How far can a Christian go?', and you can use them today.

1. WILL THIS LEAD TO FREEDOM OR SLAVERY?

'Everything is permissible for me' – but not everything is beneficial. 'Everything is permissible for me' – but I will not be mastered by anything. (1 Cor. 6:12)

The real issue, then, is not whether a thing is allowed or even approved; but, *will it make a slave out of me?* Anything that gets control over a Christian is wrong, even if others think it is right. Is playing in your local football team a sin? Er, no . . . but hang on! What about when your head is so full of winning the next match that you have no time or inclination for reading the Bible, prayer, or sharing your faith with others? What about when you give up going to church or youth group because it clashes with training? And how about girlfriends/boyfriends? No – I'm not about to go off on a 'don't date a non-Christian' rant (clearly a bad idea; that's a no-brainer)[3] but even dating a Christian girl/guy can lead to disaster if they become so all-important that Christ loses the first place in your heart.

2. IS THIS THING MAKING ME A STUMBLING BLOCK OR A STEPPING STONE?

Be careful, however, that the exercise of your freedom does not become a stumbling block to the weak. (1 Cor. 8:9 – read on to v. 13)

'Let's face it,' says Paul, 'eating dedicated meat in a heathen temple is not going to make you spiritually weak. But suppose a weaker Christian sees you there, and starts thinking they can do all kinds of things they used to think were out of order? If that person ends up sinning, you are to blame.' You see, the real issue is not what any of these practices will do to you personally, but what they will do to those who watch you. After all, you may be the only Christian they know! It's better to sacrifice the activity in question and be the best example possible than to risk the danger of making some other teenager stumble into sin. If you are genuinely free to do something, you are also free to decide not to.

Perhaps you've just turned 18. You're at a party and you get offered a drink. It's perfectly legal and it's just one. But suppose another Christian is there, and they're only 16, and you know they can't handle alcohol well. Perhaps if you decide to have a Coke instead, they won't feel the pressure to conform, and won't end up making a drunken fool of themselves – or worse.

3. WILL IT BE CONSTRUCTIVE OR DESTRUCTIVE?

'Everything is permissible' – but not everything is beneficial. 'Everything is permissible' – but not everything is constructive. (1 Cor. 10:23)

It's very easy to destroy yourself – your body, mind, memory or emotions. You have only one body, one mind, one life; take care of it. Your mates may choose to read certain magazines, or watch certain films, but if you did, they would destroy you. If you detect anything in your life – even a 'good' thing – that dulls your spiritual appetite or makes it easy to sin, then get rid of it in a hurry.

YOU DON'T HAVE TO ROB A BANK OR CHEAT ON AN EXAM TO DISCOVER THAT STEALING IS DESTRUCTIVE.

You don't have to rob a bank or cheat on an exam to discover that stealing is destructive. You don't have to visit A&E on a Friday night to know that excessive alcohol destroys your health and reputation. These things are pretty clearly covered in the Bible, as well as being obvious from other people's experiences. But when it comes to the questionable things that Christians disagree on, you'll have to test them for yourself – honestly and prayerfully – to see whether they build you up or destroy you.

4. AM I DOING THIS TO PLEASE MYSELF OR GLORIFY GOD?

So whether you eat or drink or whatever you do, do it all for the glory of God'. (1 Cor. 10:31)

As a Christian, your privilege and responsibility is to use your body to glorify and to magnify God (1 Cor. 6:20; Phil. 1:20). One famous declaration of the Christian faith states that humanity's great aim – our reason for living – is to 'glorify God and enjoy Him forever'. If what you choose to do glorifies you, bigs you up in the eyes of your friends, but minimizes, or even disgraces, your Saviour, then it's just plain wrong. End of.

THE MAKER'S GUIDELINES

You can use these four tests to think about any of the grey areas you come across on a daily basis. If whatever it is, is not explicitly forbidden and passes the four tests, then go ahead. But don't kid yourself that something's OK when it doesn't fit the Bible's principles; be perfectly honest in your dealings with God. Romans 14:5 tells us 'Each one should be fully convinced in his own mind.' In fact, take some time to read Romans 14 now as it goes over this whole issue in detail.

If you put a metal bowl in your microwave, you will trash it. Stick to the manufacturer's guidelines and you will get a nice hot meal. Similarly, the Christian teenager who honestly follows the Maker's instructions, trying to please Christ in everything, will avoid disaster and live the best sort of life.

MAKE IT REAL

Where are you most tempted to conform to the world? Be honest.

Ask the Holy Spirit to transform you as you spend time praying and reading the Bible.

Think of some specific areas where you're not sure what the 'Christian' response should be. Run it through the tests above. Does that help? Be truthful with yourself.

NOTES

1. http://bible.org/illustration/soldier-knelt-and-prayed.

2. For a great book on this idea of being a transformer not a conformer, try the brilliantly titled *Get More Like Jesus While Watching TV* by Steve Couch and Nick Pollard. (Southampton: Damaris Publishing, 2005).

3. In the New Testament we're told not to 'yoke together' with unbelievers (2 Cor. 6:14). When you're 'yoked' with someone it means pulling the same way. You simply can't pull the same way for Jesus when you're yoked with someone who doesn't believe in Him or His desires for your life. Relationships like this can cause a lot of heartache, and usually result in the Christian walking away from God.

A LIVING MIRACLE: MARY

It's 10 at night. You're bored. There's nothing on TV, it's no fun playing computer games on your own, all your mates are busy and no one is returning your texts. Even the latest online game is getting old. So you resort to the last resort of the truly desperate: updating your Facebook status. 'Bored. B.O.R.E.D. Inbox me.'

Just compare your life to Mary's for a minute.

Little or no education. No opportunity to leave your home town, which to be honest is a total dump. Becoming pregnant in your mid teens and then married off. Doesn't sound like much of a life for a teenage girl. But Mary was the happiest girl in Nazareth. She may not have had a smart phone, university offer, designer wardrobe or flatscreen TV in her bedroom, but just see how full of joy she is in Luke 1:26–56.

What was the reason for this joy? God had made her life into a miracle. It wasn't a glow that lasts for a while then wears off, or a quick thrill, but a lasting, satisfying joy. Getting great exam results, winning a match, receiving a fantastic present are all external sources of joy, and none of them last forever, but joy on the inside, joy like

Mary's, will make your life extraordinary.

There were four sources of joy in Mary's life. Let's look at them.

THE JOY OF SALVATION

Mary was a saved teenager, and this is where real joy begins. The first miracle in your life must be the miracle of salvation, of putting your faith in Jesus Christ.

Why is this a miracle? Just look at Ephesians 2:1–5.

> **As for you, you were dead in your transgressions and sins, in which you used to live when you followed the ways of this world and of the ruler of the kingdom of the air, the spirit who is now at work in those who are disobedient. All of us also lived among them at one time, gratifying the cravings of our sinful nature and following its desires and thoughts. Like the rest, we were by nature objects of wrath. But because of his great love for us, God, who is rich in mercy, made us alive with Christ even when we were dead in transgressions – it is by grace you have been saved.**

Do you see that? Once you were dead. *Dead*. A corpse cannot save itself, but if you are a Christian, God has made you alive with Christ. Every Christian is a walking, talking resurrection miracle. Have you ever realized that's what you are, and thanked God for it?

Of course, some Christians would argue that Mary didn't need to be saved, that she was in some way sinless.

Erm . . . nice theory, but look at what she herself says.

Firstly, she calls God her Saviour in Luke 1:47, and secondly, Luke reminds us of Jesus' human family tree all the way back to Adam (Luke 3:38). Every single one of Adam's descendents – you, me, Mary – is tainted by his sin. It's as if we're all carriers of the same genetic flaw. We are *all* sinners in need of a Saviour. And it's not just 'inherited sin' – can you honestly look back at the past twenty-four hours and say everything you have said, thought and done has been good? Mary was no different to the rest of us.

Why was Mary saved? Was it because she was chosen to be the special person through whom Christ would come into the world? Nope! She was saved because she trusted God's promise – just like you or me.

Ephesians 2:8,9 explains how any sinner is saved:

For it is by grace you have been saved, through faith – and this not from yourselves, it is the gift of God – not by works, so that no-one can boast.

What's grace? Grace is God's *free, unearned favour*. By grace, through faith – it's that simple. That's the way Mary was saved. The angel said to her, 'Greetings, you who are highly favoured' – the word 'favoured' is literally 'grace-d'. Later, Elizabeth says to Mary, 'Blessed is she who has believed' (v. 45). Grace and faith are the secrets of the miracle of salvation, the miracle that brings real joy.

Have you experienced this miracle? If not, why not believe God's promise and open your heart to Him? Then you will know the same joy that Mary knew: the joy of sins forgiven, the joy of being a child in God's family for ever and ever.

But there was a second joy that Mary had . . .

THE JOY OF SUBMISSION

'I am the Lord's servant,' Mary answered. 'May it be to me as you have said.' (Luke 1:38)

Submission is a difficult and costly thing. Mary willingly gave up her body, mind, and will to the control of God. In a far more conservative culture, this was *very* costly for her. As an unmarried mother she risked her forthcoming marriage, and although God graciously explained His plan to her fiancé (Matt.1:18–25), she probably faced all kinds of malicious gossip and misunderstanding (John 8:41 may have been a dig at Jesus' birth). Despite all this, Mary willingly submitted herself to God's plan.

Submission is a scary word – perhaps it makes you think of being trampled all over like a doormat, or generally having to be weak and wimpy. But you don't find Mary worrying nor complaining, do you? In fact, you find her singing! Submitting to Christ in everything brings real joy; our proud hearts and wills find it difficult, but the reward is true and lasting joy.

How do we do it, then? Is it an effort of will? If your willpower is anything like mine, then we're doomed to failure! Perhaps the most helpful way to look at is it to take a sneaky peek at Ephesians 5:21–33. Yes, yes, I know it's talking about marriage, and submission in marriage, but actually it's not just about that. It's talking about Christ and the church.

You see, the church (all Christians) submits to Christ. Why? Well, look at what he's done for us (v. 25). Jesus gave up His life for us, He loves us that much! It's not difficult to trust and submit to someone who you know loves you and always has your best interests at heart, no matter what the cost to themselves. Submitting ourselves to God is easy once we understand what He is like and what He has done for us in Christ.

So what does it look like in practice? Well, we submit ourselves to God by living by His Word, just like Mary did, 'May it be to me as you have said' (v. 38). He is in charge. Mary calls herself God's servant – she was not in charge, He was. And like Mary, it means living to glorify the Lord (v. 46). Old-fashioned Bible versions say that she 'magnifies the Lord' – her life makes Him more visible to others. Take some time to pray that God would help you to truly know Him, submit to Him, obey Him, and glorify Him in your life.

TAKE SOME TIME TO PRAY THAT GOD WOULD HELP YOU TO TRULY KNOW HIM, SUBMIT TO HIM, OBEY HIM, AND GLORIFY HIM IN YOUR LIFE.

The third joy in Mary's life was . . .

THE JOY OF THE SCRIPTURES

The amazing thing about her song in Luke 1:46–55 is that it is full of Old Testament quotations – and Mary didn't own a Bible. Ordinary people of Jesus' day didn't have copies of the Old Testament; they heard it read daily at the synagogue. Mary had never had her own youth Bible or learned memory verse songs, but she knew the Word of God and was able to quote it. In fact, her song contains quotations from the Law, the Prophets, and the Psalms, all the major parts of her Bible.

'If your Bible is falling apart, it's unlikely you are' goes the famous quote. A tad cheesy but you know what I mean. Knowing the Bible will protect you against the devil's lies (John 8:44). Eve was tempted to distrust, distort and deny God's Word back in Genesis 3. But how did Jesus respond when He faced the same temptation? Read Luke 4:1–13. Knowing and trusting God's Word helped Him defeat Satan every time – 'it is written/ says' (vv. 4,8,12).

WHAT'S THE FIRST THING YOU REACH FOR IN THE MORNING? YOUR BIBLE OR YOUR PHONE?

Mary was a joyful teenager because she hid God's Word in her heart and obeyed it in her life (Ps. 119:11). In fact, why not read the whole of Psalm 119 and list how many reasons are given to read God's Word?

Ask yourself, do I enjoy studying and obeying the Word of God? What's the first thing you reach for in the morning? Your Bible or your phone? If you were imprisoned or shipwrecked what would bring you more comfort – knowing parts of the Bible by heart, or being able to play Angry Birds? But this isn't meant to be a guilt trip – I know I'll often reach for my phone before I open my Bible. But why not try doing it the other way round? See what it's like to let God's Word and God's agenda be the first thing to shape your day.

Why not try reading just one verse or short passage each morning, thinking about it, praying about it, and then remembering it as you go to bed that night and seeing whether it had any impact on your day? Try it for a week. Or ask a youth leader how to get into reading your Bible more on your own. Or how about reading a book of the Bible with a friend? You could both read a passage, and each week spend fifteen minutes talking about it together. Maybe start with Mark's gospel or Philippians.

Behind the three joys we have already mentioned is the fourth joy . . .

THE JOY OF THE SPIRIT

A few years back there was an advertising campaign for the soft drink Sprite. The tagline was: 'Image is nothing. Thirst is everything. Obey your thirst.' I saw a church change Sprite to the Spirit – 'Image is nothing. Christ is everything. Obey your God.' That's how the Spirit helps us to live.

If you are a Christian, the Holy Spirit lives within you and has made your body His temple. His job is to make Christ real to you and to help you make Christ real to your not-yet-Christian friends (John 16:7–15). It was the Holy Spirit who overshadowed Mary and made her the mother of Christ (Luke 1:35). It was the Spirit who brought the Word to her mind and gave her a song to sing. There is no substitute for the joy of the Spirit.

It's interesting that the apostle Paul contrasts being 'under the influence' (in other words, drunk, and the buzz you get from that 'high'), with being 'under the influence' of the Spirit in Ephesians 5:18–21; an ultimately more satisfying buzz. Your non-Christian friends may enjoy the 'pleasures of sin for a short time' (Heb. 11:25) as they live for the moment. But look at what life under the influence of the Holy Spirit is like – 'May the God of hope fill you with all joy and peace as you trust in him, so that you may overflow with hope by the power of the Holy Spirit' (Rom. 15:13).

Hope for the future – the certain expectation of heaven and the deep joy of knowing God now, knowing you are loved and forgiven, that your life has meaning and purpose, beats waking up with your hundredth hangover or after yet another meaningless one-night stand. Remember Jesus promised, 'I have come that they may have life, and have it to the full' (John 10:10). God doesn't do second best.

GOD DOESN'T DO SECOND BEST.

So how can you tell if the Holy Spirit is at work in your life? Look back to Ephesians 5:18–21 and then take a look at Colossians 3:16,17. List the characteristics you find. Any similarities with Mary's response? Yep, joy, thanksgiving and submission

It's no coincidence that when the Holy Spirit is in control of a Christian's life exactly the same three characteristics are visible. When you are filled with the Spirit, you know it because you are joyful, thankful, and submissive. When you are filled with the Word of God you are joyful, thankful, and submissive! God tells us that His Word is the 'sword of the Spirit' (Eph. 6:17); the two always go together.

Have you experienced the same joy that Mary knew? Or is your life boring? Do you know the joy of salvation? Have you submitted your body, mind, and will to God, for Him to use for His glory? Do you spend time with your Bible, storing up God's Word in your heart? If so, God's Holy Spirit can transform an ordinary teenager into a living miracle.

MAKE IT REAL

It might seem a bit scary, but why not pray what Mary prayed? 'Let it be to me as You have said' or as Jesus later prayed, 'Not my will, but Yours.' Remember who created us and bought us with His own blood. Trust Him because He loves you. Spend some time now submitting yourself to God.

THE YOUNG LEADER: TIMOTHY

When the talented but troubled singer Amy Winehouse died, many magazines and blogs commented that at least she'd left behind her talented goddaughter, Dionne Bromfield. Shortly before Amy's death, Dionne commented that Amy wasn't only her godmother but her boss and her mentor. Time will tell whether Dionne turns out to be as gifted, but hopefully not as troubled, as her mentor.[1]

Do you have a mentor? If you have had someone older take an interest in you, helping you in some way, maybe in a sport or with school work, you'll know how valuable that is. If you've had the benefit in your Christian life of someone older praying or reading the Bible with you, even better!

Timothy had a great mentor – he was probably in his teens when the apostle Paul enlisted him as part of his missionary team. Not every Christian leader has time for young people, and patience to invest in them spiritually, but Paul believed in Timothy and gave him every chance to grow and prove himself in the Lord's work. Just think for a minute how our churches today could look if every mature Christian 'adopted' a 'Timothy' of their own.

As you can see from the contents page of your Bible, we have two letters that Paul wrote to Timothy. Timothy, his mother, and his grandmother (and possibly his father, but we aren't sure) lived in the area around Derbe and Lystra, probably in the city of Lystra itself. Paul visited there on his first missionary journey (Acts 14). It was at that time Lois and Eunice were saved, and then young Timothy (possibly about 7 or 8 years old). For Paul, Timothy would become his 'son in the faith' (1 Tim. 1:2).

Later on, Paul and his co-workers planted the church in Ephesus, but unfortunately, the good work they started was undermined by false teachers. So while Paul went on to found and visit other churches, he left Timothy behind to fight for the truth – that's when he wrote 1 Timothy, to encourage and help Timothy look after the church. Later on, Paul was arrested yet again for preaching the gospel, and taken to Rome. This time he didn't get out, and 2 Timothy is the last letter we have which Paul wrote.

These two letters are very personal, and when we look carefully, they seem a bit like Paul's photograph albums, looking back at his relationship with Timothy. Without much effort, you can find in these two letters at least three pictures of Timothy that illustrate what a genuine Christian he was as a teenager, and then as a young man.

Firstly . . .

TIMOTHY THE SERVANT

Just after Timothy, his mum and gran had been saved, Paul had had to leave town. And what did Timothy do? He started learning the Word of God: 'from infancy you have known the holy Scriptures,' Paul reminds him in 2 Timothy 3:15. And he also got stuck in to the local church so that by the time Paul came back to town five or six years later, he discovered that 'The brothers at Lystra and Iconium spoke well of him' (Acts 16:2).

It doesn't sound very glamorous as a preparation for becoming world famous – reading your Bible and serving in the local church. But Timothy was following the example of Jesus, 'Who, being in very nature God . . . took the very nature of a servant' (Phil. 2:6,7).

When I was a newly converted teenager, I went on a Christian summer camp as part of the student team. Our job was basically to keep the practical side of camp running – we cleaned toilets, peeled potatoes and did load of washing up. Despite this, I had a great time, made some wonderful friends and learned loads about humble service. The next summer, however, while some of my friends were 'promoted' to being dorm leaders, working with younger teenagers and doing fun activities, I was invited back to do the same thing again. 'Hang on a minute,' I thought. 'I've just been made CU rep at college. I am far too important to waste my gifts cleaning toilets.' That was exactly why I needed to spend another year doing so.

As a new Christian, you may be filled with enthusiasm and energy to get involved in all sorts of ministries, but unless that enthusiasm is backed up by spiritual knowledge and experience, you can do more harm than good. When Paul was advising Timothy on choosing church leaders at Ephesus, he tells him not to pick 'a recent convert, or he may become conceited and fall under the same judgment as the devil' and cautions that they 'must first be tested; and then if there is nothing against them, let them serve' (1 Tim. 3:6,10).

You might sometimes wonder why your church leaders don't give you important jobs or the opportunity to lead. Perhaps the reason is simple: they know you aren't ready for it yet. First you have to prove yourself, and then maybe God will open the doors for public service.

> **FIRST YOU HAVE TO PROVE YOURSELF, AND THEN MAYBE GOD WILL OPEN THE DOORS FOR PUBLIC SERVICE.**

A few verses after Paul tells the Philippian church 'look not only to your own interests, but also to the interests of others. Your attitude should be the same as that of Christ Jesus' (Phil. 2:4,5), he is able to say of Timothy that 'I have no-one else like him, who takes a genuine interest in your welfare. For everyone looks out for his own interests, not those of Jesus Christ. But you know that Timothy has proved himself, because as a son with his father he has served with me in the work of the gospel' (Phil. 2:20–22).

Secondly . . .

TIMOTHY THE SOLDIER

Paul often used military and athletic imagery – he mentions running, wrestling, boxing, and other athletic activities, as well as military terms to teach spiritual truths. Notice how he tells Timothy to 'Endure hardship with us like a good soldier of Christ Jesus' (2 Tim. 2:3).

He doesn't suggest that Timothy enlists in the army of Christ; he informs him that he is already a soldier! The Christian life isn't a playground; it's a battleground.

Expect battles. Don't go out and deliberately start them, but expect them. '. . . everyone who wants to live a godly life in Christ Jesus will be persecuted' (2 Tim. 3:12). Because you belong to Christ and live for Him, the world hates you, and so does Satan. But you can be sure that God will give you the strength you need to face the enemies and fight the battles, so 'be strong in the grace that is in Christ Jesus' (2 Tim. 2:1).

One thing that is demanded of soldiers above all else is loyalty. 'No-one serving as a soldier gets involved in civilian affairs – he wants to please his commanding officer' says 2 Timothy 2:4.

A LOYAL CHRISTIAN SOLDIER ISN'T GOING TO GET ENTANGLED WITH THE WORLD – IT WOULD MAKE THEM A TRAITOR

A loyal Christian soldier isn't going to get entangled with the world – it would make them a traitor, because the world is Christ's enemy. Paul already knew soldiers like that (2 Tim. 4:10). The Old Testament is full of similar examples – think of Samson who allowed himself (and his hair) to get entangled with the enemy, and ended up a blind prisoner in the enemy dungeon. Read Judges 16 if you've forgotten the story.

But how exactly does a Christian soldier become entangled with the world? There are three dangerous steps. Being friends with the world (Jas. 4:4), loving the world (1 John 2:15) and being conformed to the world (Rom. 12:2). We start by tolerating or even approving of the attitudes and behaviour around us, then we actually enjoy and want to act that way ourselves. Soon we look no different to anyone else.

You hang out with mates who gossip. You don't say anything because you don't want to offend them. Then a really juicy bit of gossip comes your way, and you can't wait to pass it on. Before you know it, you're gossiping as hard as the rest of them. Friends, lovers, imitators – and before the soldier knows it, they have betrayed their own Captain of Salvation.

'I have fought the good fight,' Paul wrote to Timothy at the end of his life (2 Tim. 4:7). What better record could a Christian soldier have?

Finally . . .

TIMOTHY THE STEWARD

We don't really use this word much these days, but a steward is a person who guards and invests his master's wealth. His main responsibility is to be faithful and be able to give a good report to his master.

Paul was a steward of the message of the gospel, 'the glorious gospel of the blessed God, which he entrusted to me' (1 Tim. 1:11). And what did Paul do with this priceless treasure? He, in turn, gave it to Timothy. His last words in 1 Timothy 6:20 are, 'Timothy, guard what has been entrusted to your care.' And what was Timothy to do with that sacred trust? He was to pass it on to others:

. . . the things you have heard me say in the presence of many witnesses entrust to reliable

men who will also be qualified to teach others. (2 Tim. 2:2)

God gave the treasure to Paul; Paul entrusted it to Timothy; and Timothy was to entrust it to faithful people who, in turn, would commit it to others. That is how the Word of God came to you and me. Will you pass it on?

GOD GAVE THE TREASURE TO PAUL; PAUL ENTRUSTED IT TO TIMOTHY; AND TIMOTHY WAS TO ENTRUST IT TO FAITHFUL PEOPLE WHO, IN TURN, WOULD COMMIT IT TO OTHERS. THAT IS HOW THE WORD OF GOD CAME TO YOU AND ME. WILL YOU PASS IT ON?

In *The Lord of the Rings*, there is a character called Denethor. He is the Steward of Gondor and his job is basically to keep the city and the throne for the king until he returns. But there hasn't been a king in Gondor for hundreds of years, and while some of the stewards kept their office faithfully, Denethor has grown proud. He enjoys the power and prestige and is more interested in keeping his high position than in guarding what has been entrusted to him for the true king. Despite his love of the title 'Steward of Gondor', Denethor turns out to be an unfaithful steward.

Suppose Timothy had been an unfaithful steward? Suppose he hadn't heeded Paul's warning in 2 Timothy 1:13,14?

What you heard from me, keep as the pattern of sound teaching, with faith and love in Christ Jesus. Guard the good deposit that was entrusted to you – guard it with the help of the Holy Spirit who lives in us.

What might have happened? Well, for one thing, thousands of people would never have heard the Word of God. The church Timothy served would have become weaker and weaker and finally died. What a tragedy.

Put yourself in Timothy's place, not as the pastor of a church, but as a teenager who has been given the treasure of the Christian faith. What are you doing with it? Are you guarding your faith, valuing it above everything else? Or is it just 'second-hand' faith to you? How much is your Bible worth to you? How much do you value your church, your youth group or CU, your pastor, his sermons, your Christian heritage? You are a Christian steward, and God is depending on you to guard His spiritual treasure and pass it on to others.

Pickpockets have several tried and tested techniques to rob you – distraction, playing on your compassion, even cutting your pockets or bag with a knife. One of the most popular at the moment on nights out is the 'hug and grab'; an attractive girl or guy pretending to be slightly drunk staggers over to give you a hug whilst neatly lifting your wallet at the same time. You can Google various websites to find out how to be on your guard against these tricks. It goes without saying that Satan would also like to rob you of your spiritual treasure, and he uses four main techniques to do it.

First, he tries . . .

FALSE DOCTRINE

What's doctrine? Basically, it means truths about God – '. . . evil men and impostors will go from bad to worse, deceiving and being deceived', Paul warns in 2 Timothy 3:13. If the devil can get you to read a pamphlet by some false cult, or a book by some academic who denies the truth of Word of God, or if he can introduce you to a follower of a false doctrine, then he is on the way towards stealing your treasure from you. Watch out for false doctrine, no matter who presents it. In the very next verse, Paul says, 'But as for you, continue in what you have learned and have become convinced of, because you know those from whom you learned it' (2 Tim. 3:14). Listen to your minister, your youth group leaders and your parents (if you come from a Christian home), as they ground you in the Word of God, and you will be a faithful steward, guarding the treasure from Satan's grasp.

The devil's second scam is . . .

FALSE VALUES

'For the love of money is a root of all kinds of evil. Some people, eager for money, have wandered from the faith and pierced themselves with many griefs' warns 1 Timothy 6:10. Notice it's not money that is evil but the *love* of money.

WHAT DO YOU LOVE MORE? JESUS OR MONEY?

What do you love more? Jesus or money? How will that affect working on Sunday to earn cash for the latest fashions and gadgets, but missing church? Or blowing your student loan on a party trip to Ibiza with your uni mates, which means you can't go and serve on a Christian summer camp? Or moaning to your parents because you don't have a flatscreen TV or trip to Disneyland because they are in low paid Christian ministry?

If anything in this world becomes more important to you than knowing Christ, you are in danger of losing the treasure.

Satan's third trick is . . .

FALSE KNOWLEDGE

'Timothy, guard what has been entrusted to your care. Turn away from godless chatter and the opposing ideas of what is falsely called knowledge, which some have professed and in so doing have wandered from the faith' warns 1 Timothy 6:20,21. Paul isn't criticizing true learning – God wants us to use our brains as we study the world around us – but false knowledge; the empty but popular thoughts and values of our culture.

We don't like looking stupid or intolerant. But when popular opinion goes against what the Bible teaches, it's false knowledge and we need to stick with the truth however unpopular or hated we become. And don't forget why we persevere:

Let us fix our eyes on Jesus, the author and perfecter of our faith, who for the joy set before him endured the cross, scorning its shame, and sat down at the right hand of the throne of God. Consider him who endured such opposition from sinful men, so that you will not grow weary and lose heart. In your struggle against sin, you have not yet resisted to the point of shedding your blood' (Heb. 12:2–4).

The devil's final technique is . . .

FALSE LIVING

If he can get the Christian steward to say they believe one thing but live as if it's not true, he has won the battle. '. . . fight the good fight,' Paul writes in 1 Timothy 1:18,19, 'holding on to faith and a good conscience. Some have rejected these and so have shipwrecked their faith.'

We've all heard about the *Titanic*, and how by going at full speed against the iceberg warnings, the captain indirectly caused the most famous and tragic shipwreck of the last 100 years. Well, the fastest way to wreck your spiritual life is to go against your conscience, the inner guide God has given you to let you know when you've done something wrong. Your conscience is a delicate thing and can be easily changed from a good conscience to a corrupted conscience (Titus 1:15), then a seared conscience that no longer functions (1 Tim. 4:2). If you badly burn your hand (or 'sear' it) you lose all feeling in that hand. Likewise, if you keep going against your conscience – lying to your parents, sleeping with your boyfriend, watching that porn on your phone – you will eventually stop feeling your conscience telling you what is right and wrong.

The Christian who does not live out what they claim to believe, who hides secret sins in their heart and practices them when they think they can get away with it, is an unfaithful steward. Before long Satan takes the treasure away. You are left empty-handed, with nothing to pass on to others.

'I have kept the faith' Paul testified in his last letter from that Roman prison (2 Tim. 4:7). He was a faithful steward – as was Timothy, his son in the faith. Will you be?

MAKE IT REAL

How are you serving other Christians? If you're not, how could you?

How are you tempted to love the world? Ask for God's help to love Jesus more.

Do you ever share your faith with other people? If you're not sure what you would say, why not practise talking about what Jesus means to you?

What tactic does the devil use most successfully to try to derail your faith? Think about it carefully, and ask for God's protection in that area.

NOTE
1. *Evening Standard ES magazine*: http://www.thisislondon.co.uk/lifestyle/esmagazine/soul-sister-dionne-bromfield-6429627.html

THE PERFECT
TEENAGER: JESUS

In the third instalment of the *High School Musical*
franchise, Ms Darbus asks her students what their plans
for the future are. Their replies range from becoming
president of the United States to staging the perfect
prom, including the inevitable desire of one of them to
be centre-stage for the rest of her life!

Stop and think for a minute about the last few films you
saw featuring teenagers. If you pick the 'classic' teenage
film from any decade from the eighties onwards, the
main ambition of its characters seems to be to have
sex, get drunk, score some drugs and/or go on a road
trip involving all three. But is that it? Is that the best a
teenager can aim for? Is that all people expect of you?
Rather insulting, isn't it?

Alex and Brett Harris, who were 16 when they founded
the popular teen site www.therebelution.com put it like
this:

> **Isn't it ironic that many teenagers, though
> fluent in multiple computer languages (we're
> considered trendsetters and early adopters
> [of new technology]), are not expected to**

understand or care about things like personal finances, politics or our faith? We're not even expected to be capable of carrying on an intelligent conversation with an adult.[1]

So, how do you change the world? Well, the best place to start is by taking a look at the teenager who *did* change the world. He didn't go on any chaos-filled road trips or end up on the world stage, or any other kind of stage.

We don't get much information about Christ's teenage years in the New Testament, but we do get a snapshot in Luke 2:39–52. Go ahead and read it. Jesus was 12 years old, just about to enter His teenage years, on the verge of His Bar Mitzvah at 13 when He would technically become a 'man'; an adult in that society. So what was His life like?

Well, He grew up in a small town with a naff reputation. And He was from a poor family (Luke 2:24 tells us that Joseph was too poor to bring a lamb or a goat for a sacrifice when Jesus was a baby; instead, he brought the cheapest option, a pair of doves or pigeons). But somehow you can't imagine Jesus moaning because His

THE LAST THING JESUS IS, IS BORING.

parents couldn't afford the latest trainers, can you? And we know from His later years that when He embarked on the work God had for Him, that His brothers and sisters didn't believe Him (John 7:1–5 and Mark 6:1 –5), and His mother, Mary, didn't always understand either (Mark 3:31–35). But I doubt that Jesus ever slammed the door to His bedroom shouting, 'No one in this house understands me!'

'Oh well, Jesus was perfect,' you might be thinking. 'Perfect but boring.' But the last thing Jesus is, is boring. If you know Him personally today, you know that He is wonderful, wise, caring, powerful and exciting. So He must have been the ideal teenager, the perfect teenager. The genuine teenager. What does that look like?

Well, in Luke 2:39–52 we see that the 12-year-old Jesus *loved the Bible, loved God* and *loved His parents*. And that He was loved by those around Him (v. 52).

Jesus would probably have been taught the Jewish Scriptures (our Old Testament) from the age of about 6 in His local synagogue. He had obviously taken them to heart, committed them to memory and let them shape His life so much that by the age of 12 He was astounding and confounding the top religious experts of His day (Luke 2:46,47). Later on in His ministry when He faced temptation by the devil, He was able to resist because He knew the Bible and used it to defend Himself. Paul doesn't call the Word of God the sword of the Spirit for nothing (Eph. 6:17).

JUST STOP FOR A MINUTE. IF YOU ARE BLESSED ENOUGH TO HAVE BEEN BROUGHT UP BY CHRISTIAN PARENTS, THANK GOD FOR THAT.

Just stop for a minute. If you are blessed enough to have been brought up by Christian parents, thank God for that. Like Timothy 'from infancy you have known the holy Scriptures, which are able to make you wise for salvation through faith in Christ Jesus' (2 Tim. 3:15). Every memory verse or song you have learned from your mum and dad or gran or junior church leader or someone else has given you access to the most important truth in the world. Being brought up as a Christian doesn't make you one – you need to make that choice for yourself. But you have been surrounded by all the information you need to be saved. Don't ever despise that privilege.

A guy named Don Carson writes this about his mother:

My mother died of Alzheimer's disease, over nine years. Nine or ten months before she died, you'd get a small flicker from the eyes or squeeze of the hand if you held up pictures of her grandchildren. Six months before she died, if you sang an old hymn like 'Blessed assurance, Jesus is mine', you'd get a squeeze. Or a quote from the King James Version that she'd been brought up on. That was about the last thing that produced any response in her. The most deeply embedded memories in that decaying brain were those old hymns and memorised Scripture.[2]

If you grow up as Jesus did, loving the Bible, memorizing it and thinking about it, wouldn't it be wonderful to think that that would be what stayed with you even at the very end of your life?

But Jesus didn't just *love the Bible* – He loved the Bible because it told Him all about God, and *He loved His heavenly Father!* When He goes AWOL in Luke 2 – and isn't it encouraging to think that even Jesus got told off by His parents? – He does it because He wants to be in His Father's house (v. 49). The Temple was where God's presence on earth was to be found, and Jesus wanted to be with His Father. Do you know that psalm that says 'Better is one day in your courts than a thousand elsewhere' (Ps. 84:10)? As we read on into Jesus' adult life, we see Him spending hours praying to His Father, spending time enjoying that relationship. If we reduce prayer to a duty or a to-do list, we miss the point. Jesus loved His Father and that's why He loved spending time talking to Him. You're blessed – you don't need to trek to Jerusalem to be close to God. Take a look at Hebrews 10:19–22:

> **Therefore . . . since we have confidence to enter the Most Holy Place by the blood of Jesus, by a new and living way opened for us through the curtain, that is, his body, and since we have a great priest over the house of God, let us draw near to God with a sincere heart in full assurance of faith, having our hearts sprinkled to cleanse us from a guilty conscience and having our bodies washed with pure water.**

Why not take advantage of what Jesus has done for you and spend some time with your heavenly Father now?

But even with all the knowledge and wisdom Jesus had, even though He longed to hang out in the Temple to be close to His Father, *Jesus still loved and obeyed His earthly parents*. Does that surprise you? Verse 51 isn't what we necessarily expect. After all, later in His life when Jesus' family try to dissuade Him from His task (and even think He's gone crazy), He ignores them and carries on with His mission (see Mark 3:21,32–35). But while Jesus is a boy, He returns home with Mary and Joseph and obeys them. Now, that might be hard to hear. We don't always want to be obedient to our parents. They might be unreasonable, they might be demanding, they might not even be Christians. But the Bible is clear; God wants us to honour and obey them (Eph. 6:1; Col. 3:20). Of course, notice that we are to obey our parents 'in the Lord', as Ephesians 6:1 says. So if your mum and dad are encouraging you to help out in the family drug-smuggling business, it's OK to say no! But we do need to honour and respect our parents. That can be very hard sometimes, but Jesus did it and He will help you.

Just a quick warning here. Have you ever sung *Once in Royal David's City* at Christmas? The lyrics urge us to grow up just like Jesus. It all sounds a bit saccharine. Jesus isn't just an example to follow – if that's all we think He is about, then we've lost the plot. Jesus didn't primarily come so we could imitate Him. His childhood, His whole life, was building up to His death. Yes, we can learn from His life, but if that's all we're focusing on, we're missing the big picture. Admiring a firefighter's uniform or shiny new fire engine is going to be of limited value if you're stuck in a burning building.

JESUS CAME TO DO WHAT WE COULD NOT DO – SAVE OURSELVES.

Jesus came to do what we could not do – save ourselves. Once we've accepted His rescue, once we've been born again (see John 3:1–8) [3] the amazing transformation begins – God's Holy Spirit starts to make us like Christ. Then we can start to imitate Him, but it's the way that a child imitates their father or older brother; we are now part of God's family, and a family likeness is beginning to emerge. If you've ever seen a newborn baby you may have heard people saying, 'Ooh, isn't he (or she) like his mum/dad?' Let's be frank, most babies look small, bald and grumpy. But when kids get older, or even as adults, you can clearly see the family resemblance. Think about celebs and their children – Shiloh Jolie-Pitt looks just like her dad. Prince William looks like his mum. Lourdes is the spitting image of the young Madonna. This natural family resemblance is a million miles away from me trying to imitate the world's best footballer – my total lack of hand-eye coordination would make that attempt doomed to failure. We don't try our best to copy Jesus – Jesus brings us into His family, and His Spirit helps us to grow up to be like Christ.

JESUS IS OUR PERFECT ELDER BROTHER, AND WE CAN DEFINITELY LEARN FROM HIM.

If you've got an older brother, maybe you watched him learn to drive, or pass his exams, and picked up a few tips. Maybe he passed on some advice about school or the opposite sex. Jesus is our perfect elder brother, and we can definitely learn from Him, as well as growing to be like Him. Don't forget that that is God's ultimate wonderful plan for you, and He can and will do it:

For those God foreknew he also predestined to be conformed to the likeness of his Son, that he might be the firstborn among many brothers. (Rom. 8:29)

And:

**'being confident of this, that he who began a
good work in you will carry it on to completion
until the day of Christ Jesus. (Phil. 1:6)**

God is planning to make you like His Son, and like the
Mastermind catchphrase, 'I've started, so I'll finish', He
will do it. That's a guarantee.

MAKE IT REAL

Dear Father God,

Thank You that You sent Your Son Jesus to live the
perfect life that I never could. Thank You that He came
to die in my place to pay the penalty for the way I ignore
You and live my way, not Yours. Thank You that by Your
Holy Spirit I can be 'born again', becoming a child in Your
family. Please enable me to grow up to be like Jesus by
the power of Your Holy Spirit. Amen.

NOTES

1. Alex and Brett Harris, *Do Hard Things*, chapter 3, 'The Myth of Adolescence'
(Colorado Springs, CO: Waterbrook Multnomah, 2008), p. 41.

2. D.A. Carson and Tony Paine, 'Is the Church a House of Worship?' *The Briefing*, Issue 232,
14 March 2000.

3. If you are puzzled about what it means to be born again, it's about asking Jesus to come
into your life as your Saviour and Lord. Ask your youth leader or a trusted Christian friend,
or email the author c/o info@10ofthose.com.

LIVE IT OUT

You must have seen the classic 'training montage' in films. Whether it's *Rocky, Legally Blonde, The Karate Kid, The Princess Diaries* or *The Incredibles*, every film that charts the development of its hero has one. It might be focused on sporting prowess or be more 'make-over'-led, but it starts with the hero being weak, clumsy and generally hopeless, and through a series of training exercises/shots of hard study/beauty treatments, eventually reveals them at the peak of their game. All to a suitably upbeat tune, of course.

So what has this got in common with the Christian life? Everything. Paul would have been a big fan of the training montage (see 1 Cor. 9:25,26). You see, you are closer to the 'before' picture in the training montage that you'd like to think. God has got more to do in you than through you. Take a look at Philippians 2:12,13:

work out your salvation with fear and trembling, for it is God who works in you to will and to act according to his good purpose.

Of course, Paul is not saying, 'Work *for* your own salvation; Nobody can work *for* salvation; Christ finished that work on the cross. Salvation does not mean that Christ made the down payment and we keep up the instalments by our own works. Nope, when Jesus said,

'It is finished' (John 19:30) on the cross, it was the same Greek word (*tetelestai*) that was stamped across final bill payments: 'Paid in full.' So 'work out your salvation' means 'fulfil in your Christian life the purpose for which you were saved'. In Ephesians 2:10, Paul says:

For we are God's workmanship, created in Christ Jesus to do good works, which God prepared in advance for us to do.

We've seen that God has a perfect plan for your life; a plan to make you into the person you were created to be, and a plan to bring Him glory. Way back in the Old Testament, God spoke to His people about His purposes, and while the specifics were for Israel at that time, He is the same God today:

'For I know the plans I have for you,' declares the Lord, 'plans to prosper you and not to harm you, plans to give you hope and a future.' (Jer. 29:11)

But this plan of God's isn't something you and I try to 'work out' on our own; it's something we work out *as God works in us. Remember: God cannot work through you until first He works in you.* He works in; we work out.

The big question at this point is: How does God work in you? And the answer is: Through His Holy Spirit. But that raises another question: How does the Holy Spirit work in you? That's the question we're going to spend the rest of this chapter looking at.

The Holy Spirit rarely works in a vacuum; He always uses *everyday means* to do His work in your life. If you were to lock yourself in your room and plead with the Spirit to make your life a miracle, all the while ignoring the tools that He uses, you'd be asking for a nervous breakdown or a satanic substitute for real spirituality. (Don't forget that the devil is an imitator, and that getting you to live on shallow emotions and false feelings is one of his most effective tricks. When the feeling wears out, your dedication is gone, and you're discouraged.)

So what tools does the Holy Spirit use to work in our lives? The big three are *prayer, the Bible* and *suffering*, and we've seen all three of them in the lives of the Bible teenagers we've looked at so far.

PRAYER

What do you think prayer is all about? The Bible describes it many ways: talking to our Father (Luke 11:2), a chance to share our anxieties, ask for our needs and give thanks (Phil. 4:6) or even an act of spiritual warfare (Eph. 6:18). But it is invariably Spirit-filled. It is God who helps us to pray:

> **. . . the Spirit helps us in our weakness. We do not know what we ought to pray for, but the Spirit himself intercedes for us with groans that words cannot express. And he who searches our hearts knows the mind of the Spirit, because the Spirit intercedes for the saints in accordance with God's will. (Rom. 8:26,27)**

Have you ever noticed that the people God uses are people who pray? Even as a teenager, Daniel prayed daily; a habit he continued all his life (Dan. 6:10,11). David certainly knew how to pray; in fact, many of the psalms are prayers he lifted to God in times of trouble and triumph. Mary's song in Luke 1:46–55 is a kind of prayer. Jesus prayed, and taught His disciples to pray. The Christian who prays daily is inviting the Spirit to work in their life.

Of course, this needs to be genuine prayer. I don't mean long and wordy – Jesus said, 'when you pray, do not keep on babbling like pagans, for they think they will be heard because of their many words' (Matt. 6:7), but equally, genuine prayer isn't rushed or mechanical.

LISTEN TO GOD'S WORD: READ IT, HEAR IT, BELIEVE IT AND ACT ON IT. MEMORIZE IT AND LIVE IT. THE HOLY SPIRIT WILL USE IT TO CHANGE YOU AND MAKE YOU MORE LIKE JESUS.

You're not alone if you find this challenging. Even Jesus' disciples had to ask Him to teach them to pray (Luke 11:1). Worthwhile things aren't easy. Two useful tools people have found helpful in structuring their prayers are 'Sorry, Thank You, Please' or ACTS – Adoration, Confession, Thanksgiving, Supplication (i.e. asking for things). Of course, you can't go far wrong if you follow the Lord's Prayer and make it your own (Matt. 6:9–13).[1]

THE BIBLE

God not only works in your life through prayer; He also works through the Bible. You might have heard it said that 'the pen is mightier than the sword', meaning that words have more power to change things than armies, and history has certainly shown that to be true.

God's Word is even more powerful. Paul calls the Bible,

'the sword of the Spirit' in Ephesians 6:17. The same metaphor appears in Hebrews 4:12:

For the Word of God is living and active. Sharper than any doubled-edged sword, it penetrates even to dividing soul and spirit, joints and marrow; it judges the thoughts and attitudes of the heart.

Have you ever read a bit of the Bible or heard it taught at church or on camp and felt that God was speaking directly to your situation? Sometimes it's the uncomfortable feeling that there's something you need to get rid of in your life, or something you need to change. Sometimes it's an encouragement to live for Jesus, a reminder of how much He loves you, and the riches of His favour and power. The Holy Spirit is using His sword to prick your conscience, to work in you.

Listen to God's Word: read it, hear it, believe it and act on it. Memorize it and live it. The Holy Spirit will use it to change you and make you more like Jesus.

SUFFERING

The third tool the Spirit uses to work in your life is suffering. 1 Peter 4:12–14 puts it this way:

Dear friends, do not be surprised at the painful trial you are suffering, as though something strange were happening to you. But rejoice that you participate in the sufferings of Christ, so that you may be overjoyed when his glory is revealed. If you are insulted because of the name

**of Christ, you are blessed, for the Spirit of glory
and of God rests on you.**

The Holy Spirit works in your life when you allow God
to put you through uncomfortable circumstances for
Christ's *sake*. This doesn't mean that the Spirit works
when you suffer because of sin (the following verses
make that abundantly clear). It does mean, however,
that God uses the furnace of suffering to melt and purify
you so that He can mould you into a Christian who will
glorify Him.

**. . . now for a little while you may have had to
suffer grief in all kinds of trials. These have come
so that your faith – of greater worth than gold,
which perishes even though refined by fire – may
be proved genuine and may result in praise,
glory and honour when Jesus Christ is revealed.
(1 Pet. 1:6,7)**

If you're not an expert in precious metals, this idea of
furnaces or fiery ordeals might seem a bit odd or scary.
Basically, it's the same technique that we use when we
recycle mobile phones. After all the salvageable bits have
been stripped from your old handset, the remaining
components are sent to a precious metals recovery
facility where precious and base metals are extracted
using a furnace. The different metals have different
melting temperatures so it's easy to separate the valuable
ones from the rest.

Your 'furnace' might be being given a hard time or
being laughed at by the crowd at school; or maybe being
misunderstood and maligned by non-Christian friends
and family. It's not much fun at the time, but if you are

'insulted because of the name of Christ' (1 Pet. 4:14), you can be sure that the Spirit will be there to work in your life and give you joy in the midst of suffering.

Why not take a look at some of these verses (there are many others) and store them away in your memory? When suffering comes, you can be sure that they will be a huge comfort and encouragement to you.

Psalm 46:1; Isaiah 43:1,2; Matthew 5:10–12; 2 Timothy 3:12; 1 Peter 2:19–25

WORKING IN AND THROUGH YOU

You can see, then, how the Spirit works in you: suffering, God's Word and prayer. Joseph was unjustly imprisoned for years. David was on the run in fear of his life. Daniel faced lions. Mary risked her future marriage and reputation. Timothy faced opposition. But they all trusted God's Word, they all held onto His promises, and they prayed. God's Spirit was at work in them, and He did great things through them.

God wants to work *through* you, but He can't work *through* you until He first works *in* you. He is more concerned about what you are than about what you do, because if your Christian character is right, your service will be right. If you spend time daily with your Bible, if you have a consistent prayer life, and if you trust God in whatever circumstances He brings into your life, then He will be able to work *in* and *through* you for His glory.

If you're thinking 'this all seems like a lot of hard work', then, you'd be right. But remember who it is that is working hard. Our God and King:

May God himself, the God of peace, sanctify you through and through. May your whole spirit, soul and body be kept blameless at the coming of our Lord Jesus Christ. The one who calls you is faithful and he will do it. (1 Thess. 5:23,24)

MAKE IT REAL

How easy/difficult do you find it to read your Bible? What helps you? There are some great resources out there like *Engage* by Martin Cole, published by The Good Book Company.

Do you have a regular time when you pray? Some junior doctors are so busy they hardly get a chance to eat, so they take a minute to pray when they go to the toilet. It means they keep talking to God and asking for His help throughout the day.

Why not decide to pray or read the Bible regularly with a Christian friend?

Look back at those verses about suffering. Why not learn one or two off by heart – it won't take as long as your times tables and will be even more useful!

NOTE

1. Some great books on prayer include Douglas Kelly's *If God Already Knows Why Pray?* (Tain: Christian Focus, 1995).

77

THE GENUINE ARTICLE

In the film *Chicken Run*, a community of chickens are imprisoned in a World War Two-style prison camp. The evil Mrs Tweedy makes the decision to change the farm's focus from egg production (where poor layers get the chop) to chicken pies. The morning after she makes this decision, the chickens are fed more generously than they have ever been before. They hurl themselves at the feeding troughs, fighting to eat as much as possible. Only Ginger, their leader, yells 'Stop!' She can see what is happening – they are being fattened for slaughter.

If you have got this far, then you are Ginger! You have seen through the world's attempts to make you a fake teenager through advertising, peer pressure and all kinds of temptations.

You know the stakes, you understand the pressures, but you also know that God has a purpose for your life. Just think back to the Bible teenagers we've looked at. They were

THEY WERE REAL PEOPLE WITH REAL STRUGGLES, BUT BECAUSE GOD WAS AT WORK IN THEIR LIVES THEY HAVE LOTS TO TEACH US. MOST OF ALL, BECAUSE GOD WAS AT WORK IN THEM, THEY POINT US TO JESUS.

real people with real struggles, but because God was at work in their lives they have lots to teach us. Most of all, because God was at work in them, they point us to Jesus.

Joseph learned about service, self-control and suffering, just like our Lord Jesus who 'did not come to be served, but to serve, and to give his life as a ransom for many' (Mark 10:45).

David began with hard work, serving faithfully in a low position, and ended up as a king. Jesus

. . . being in very nature God,
did not consider equality with God
something to be grasped,
but made himself nothing,
taking the very nature of a servant,
being made in human likeness.
And being found in appearance as a man,
he humbled himself
and became obedient to death – even
death on a cross!
Therefore God exalted him to the highest place
and gave him the name that is above every
name,
that at the name of Jesus every knee
should bow,
in heaven and on earth and under the earth,
and every tongue confess that Jesus Christ is
Lord,
to the glory of God the Father. (Phil. 2:6–11)

Daniel stayed faithful to God and refused to conform to the pressure of the world around him, just as Jesus refused to take the easy way out in the garden of Gethsemane: 'Father, if you are willing, take this cup from me; yet not my will, but yours be done' (Luke 22:42).

Mary knew the joy of being saved, of submitting herself to God, and knowing God's Spirit at work in her as she listened to the Bible. We've also seen how her Son loved spending time with His Father in prayer and let God's Word set His priorities.

And Timothy imitated Paul just as Paul imitated Jesus (1 Thess. 1:6; 1 Cor. 4:15–17), being a faithful servant, soldier and steward.

The book of Hebrews brilliantly describes how we should see all these believers who have lived before us. These 'witnesses', these Bible teenagers, faced the same trials and temptations you do, but they also knew God's guiding presence with them, and had the same glorious future to look forward to:

Therefore, since we are surrounded by such a great cloud of witnesses, let us throw off everything that hinders and the sin that so easily entangles, and let us run with perseverance the race marked out for us. Let us fix our eyes on Jesus, the author and perfecter of our faith, who for the joy set before him endured the cross, scorning its shame, and sat down at the right hand of the throne of God. (Heb. 12:1,2)

Running at the Olympics in a vast stadium filled with

your supporters might be your dream come true, or your worst nightmare, but this race isn't dependent on our sporting ability. The stadium is full of believers like these Bible teenagers who have already finished the race. All you have to do is follow Jesus, who has run the race ahead of you and whose Spirit is running alongside you, helping you. The gold medal has already got your name on it!

In *Chicken Run*, the chickens eventually escape. They suffer hardships, they serve each other and they work together, but they get to live in freedom as *genuine* chickens, not just battery farmed pie-fillings.

So, likewise, be a *genuine* teenager! Be the person you were created to be, the person you were bought by Jesus' blood to be. A fake Rolex looks good for a while, but soon breaks. The genuine article lasts a lifetime. Be genuine!

THE GOLD MEDAL HAS ALREADY GOT YOUR NAME ON IT!

10 Publishing

a division of **10** of those.com

10Publishing is the publishing house of **10ofThose**. It is committed to producing quality Christian resources that are biblical and accessible.

www.10ofthose.com is our online retail arm selling thousands of quality books at discounted prices. We also service many church bookstalls and can help your church to set up a bookstall. Single and bulk purchases welcome.

For information contact: **sales@10ofthose.com** or check out our website: **www.10ofthose.com**